Meet the people that look after me

Zoologist

the
BIG
PICTURE

Louise Spilsbury

Published 2010 by
A&C Black Publishers Ltd.
36 Soho Square, London, W1D 3QY

www.acblack.com

ISBN HB 978-1-4081-2796-4
      PB 978-1-4081-3150-3

Text copyright © 2010 Louise Spilsbury

The right of Louise Spilsbury to be identified as the author of this work has been asserted by her in accordance with the Copyrights, Designs and Patents Act 1988.

A CIP catalogue for this book is available from the British Library.

Every effort has been made to trace copyright holders and to obtain their permission for use of copyright material. The author and publishers would be pleased to rectify any error or omission in future editions.

This book is produced using paper that is made from wood grown in managed, sustainable forests. It is natural, renewable and recyclable. The logging and manufacturing processes conform to the environmental regulations of the country of origin.

Produced for A&C Black by Calcium. www.calciumcreative.co.uk

Printed and bound in China by C&C Offset Printing Co.

All the internet addresses given in this book were correct at the time of going to press. The author and publishers regret any inconvenience caused if addresses have changed or sites have ceased to exist, but can accept no responsibility for any such changes.

Acknowledgements

The publishers would like to thank the following for their kind permission to reproduce their photographs:

Cover: Shutterstock: Tischenko Irina (front), Alle (back). **Pages:** Fotolia: Kitch Bain 21, Fabrice Beauchene 15, Kirubeshwaran 12-13, Andrea Riva 16-17; Istockphoto: Marcel Pelletier 6-7; Shutterstock: Petrov Andrey 12, Kitch Bain 1, Braam Collins 18-19, Lucian Coman 2-3 (background), 5, David Dea 22-23, Tiago Jorge da Silva Estima 24, Eric Isselée 7, Kwest 4-5, Milos Markovic 20-21, Christian Musat 3, Nik Niklz 14-15, Dr. Morley Read 19, Szefei 8, Aaron Welch 11, Brooke Whatnall 4, Worldswildlifewonders 8-9, Ximagination 16, Ludmila Yilmaz 10-11.

Contents

A Zoologist

Zoologists are people who study different animals all around the world.

All about animals

Zoologists learn about where animals live, what they eat, and how they get their food.

This zoologist is finding out about koala bears.

Cute!

Wild side

Zoologists study animals in zoos and in the wild. Some animals attack people if they feel scared. Zoologists try not to frighten them.

Sssscary!

At the Zoo

Some zoologists are zookeepers. They care for animals in zoos.

Happy animals

Zookeepers make sure animals eat healthily. They put rocks, ponds, and trees around the animals to make them feel at home.

Bathtime!

In danger

Some animals are in danger in the wild. In zoos, these animals can be well looked after and have babies. This will hopefully stop them from dying out.

Panda mums and babies can be cared for in a zoo.

7

In Rainforests

Rainforests are huge forests with very tall trees. They are found in hot and wet places.

Up high, down low

Zoologists study animals that live on the rainforest floor, such as **jaguars**. They also study birds and other animals that live up in the trees.

Colourful birds called toucans live in rainforests.

Gone forever?

Zoologists are worried about rainforest animals. A lot of rainforest trees are being chopped down. If rainforest animals lose their home, they may die out.

We need trees!

In Grasslands

Grasslands are places covered with tall grasses. Zoologists study how animals survive **here.**

Sneaky hunters

Animals such as lions and cheetahs have fur that blends in with grass. This helps them sneak up on **prey**, such as zebras and deer.

Can you see me?

Poo clue

One way to tell where grassland animals have been is to check out their poo! If it is fresh and smelly, it means the animal has only just left.

Animals also check out poo to tell if another animal is near.

11

In Deserts

Zoologists also visit deserts. These are the hottest places on Earth and are covered in sand.

No rain, no water?

It hardly ever rains in deserts, so zoologists study how animals here get water. Most get water from their food.

Some desert rats can turn their wee back into water. Handy!

Keeping cool

Many desert animals, such as **scorpions**, stay underground or in the shade in the day. They only come out at night, when it is cooler.

I'm cool!

13

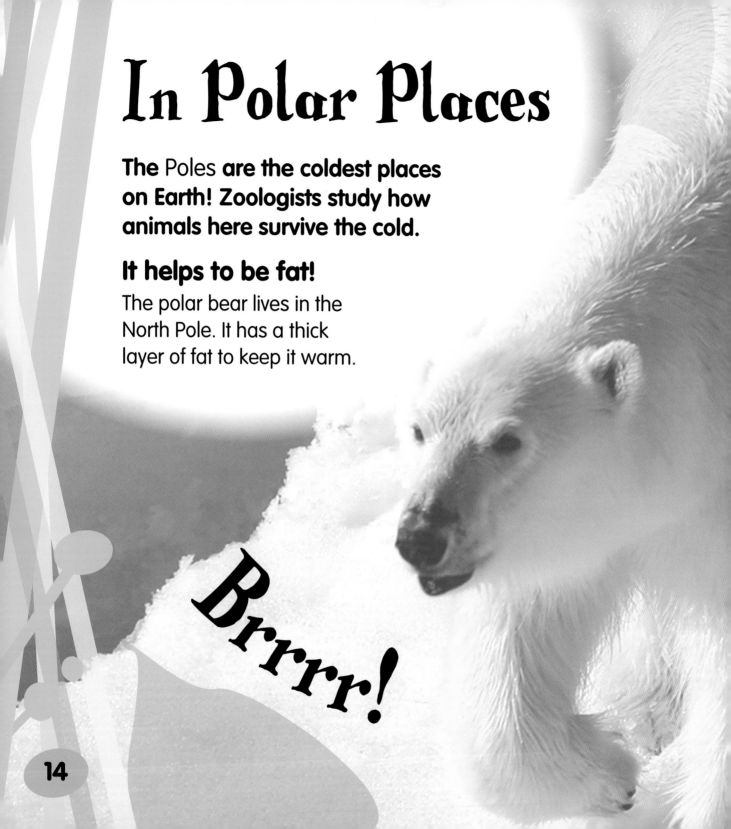

In Polar Places

The Poles are the coldest places on Earth! Zoologists study how animals here survive the cold.

It helps to be fat!

The polar bear lives in the North Pole. It has a thick layer of fat to keep it warm.

Brrrr!

Egg warming

Emperor penguins live at the South Pole. The males keep the female's eggs warm by holding them on their feet until they **hatch**.

Penguins cuddle their babies to keep them warm.

Baby

15

In Oceans

Zoologists travel in submarines, **swim in diving suits, or float in cages to study ocean animals.**

On the menu?

Some zoologists study what ocean animals eat and how they find their food.

Sharks hunt fish and other ocean animals for food.

Save some fish for us!

Fishy facts

Zoologists are worried about ocean animals. Fishing boats are taking too many fish from the oceans. Soon there may not be enough left for ocean animals to eat.

In the Lab

Some zoos study animals in labs. A lab is a room where zoologists carry out tests.

Animal hospital

Zoologists take care of sick animals in the lab. They often give them an **injection** to make them go to sleep before treating them.

Zzzzzzzzzz

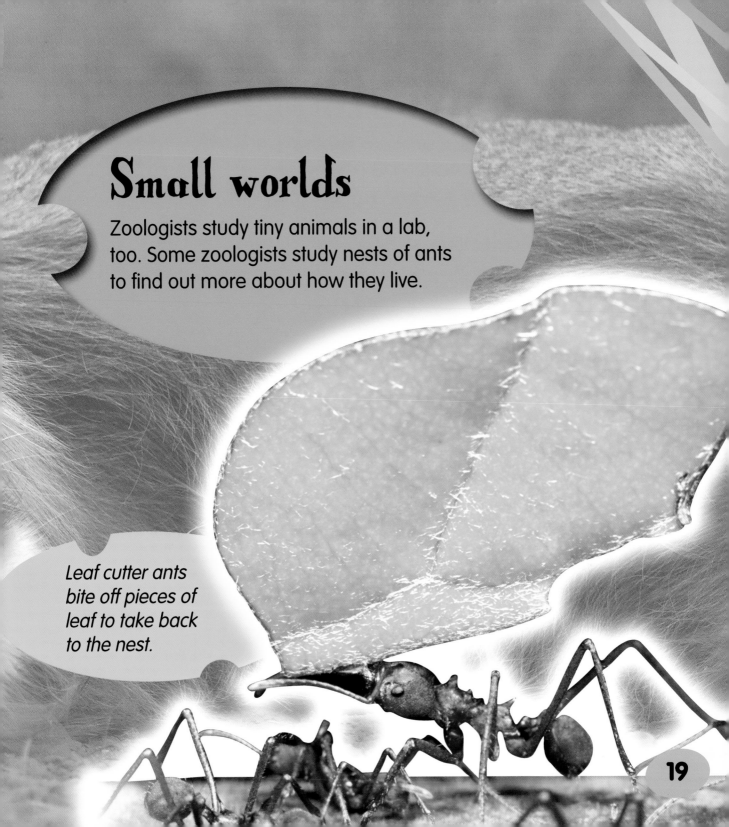

Small worlds

Zoologists study tiny animals in a lab, too. Some zoologists study nests of ants to find out more about how they live.

Leaf cutter ants bite off pieces of leaf to take back to the nest.

Be a Zoologist

If you love animals, you might want to become a zoologist.

Look and learn

Start to study the animals around you. Watch them in your garden or in a park. Draw the animals and write down what they do.

Zoologists can study and help animals in the wild.

Keep it wild

If you love being outside, being a zoologist is a great job. And best of all, you can find out how to help animals everywhere.

Hang out with us!

Glossary

hatch when a baby animal breaks out of its shell

injection medicine given through a needle

jaguars large, spotted wild cats

Poles places at the ends of the Earth where it is very cold. The North Pole is at the top and the South Pole is at the bottom of the Earth.

prey an animal that is caught and eaten by other animals

scorpions insects with large claws and a deadly sting in their tails

submarines boats that travel underwater

survive being able to stay alive

Further Reading

Websites

Find out more about zoologists at:
www.nhm.ac.uk/kids-only/ologist/zoologist

Discover amazing animals at:
http://animals.nationalgeographic.co.uk/animals

Learn more about wildlife at:
www.bbc.co.uk/nature/animals

Books

First Animal Encyclopedia (DK First Reference Series)
by Penelope Arlon, Dorling Kindersley (2004).

Animal Picture Atlas by Hazel Maskell,
Usborne Publishing (2008).

National Geographic Encyclopedia of Animals
by Karen McGhee and George McKay,
National Geographic Society (2006).

Index